How A CEO Can Prepare For

A Successful Negotiation

What You Need To Do BEFORE A Negotiation Starts In Order To Get The Best Possible Outcome

"Practical, proven techniques that will help you to become a better CEO"

Dr. Jim Anderson

Published by:
Blue Elephant Consulting
Tampa, Florida

Printed in the United States of America

ISBN-13: 978-1518683756

ISBN-10: 1518683754

Warning – Disclaimer

The purpose of this book is to educate and entertain. This book does not promise or guarantee that anyone following the ideas, tips, suggestions, techniques or strategies will be successful. The author, publisher and distributor(s) shall have neither liability nor responsibility to anyone with respect to any loss or damage caused, or alleged to be caused, directly or indirectly by the information contained in this book.

Acknowledgements

Any book like this one is the result of years of real-world work experience. In my over 25 years of working for 7 different firms, I have met countless fantastic people and I've been mentored by some truly exceptional ones. Although I've probably forgotten some of the people who made me the person that I am today, here is my attempt to finally give them the recognition that they so truly deserve:

- Thomas P. Anderson
- Art Puett
- Bobbi Marshall
- Bob Boggs

Dr. Jim Anderson

This book is dedicated to my wife Lori. None of this would have been possible without her love and support.

Thanks for the best 24 years of my life (so far)...!

Blue
Elephant
Consulting

Speaking.   Negotiating.   Managing.   Marketing.

Table Of Contents

How Does A CEO Plan A Negotiation?

It turns out that most negotiations are over even before they begin. The executive team that has spent the most time planning for the negotiation, doing their homework, and collecting the data that they'll need is the one that's going to walk away from the table with the best deal. Wouldn't you want that executive team to be your team?

Planning is what happens before a CEO sits down at the negotiating table. There are no negotiating tactics or tricks at play here. It's just a matter of you doing your homework. At the same time you hope that the other side is NOT doing their homework so that you'll show up at the negotiation more prepared then they are.

Just committing to doing the planning that your next negotiation is going to require is not enough, you also have to know just exactly how to go about doing it. That's what this book is going to teach you. Every senior level negotiation is different and so the planning that you'll have to do for every negotiation will be different also.

The planning that is required for a successful negotiation takes on many different forms. These can include planning where and when the negotiations will be held, what concessions you'll be willing to make to the other side, and understanding who has what power in the negotiations.

The end result of doing the planning that a negotiation requires is that when you sit down at the negotiating table, you'll have a sense of being prepared. You'll know what you need to know about the other side of the table, what their goals are, what their constraints are, and what they hope to be able to get out of the negotiations. This is exactly the type of knowledge that every CEO is going to need in order to be able to reach the type of deal that will allow you to walk away from the table with a sense of accomplishment.

Good luck!

- Dr. Jim Anderson

About The Author

I must confess that I never set out to be a negotiator. When I went to school, I studied Computer Science and thought that I'd get a nice job programming and that would be that. Well, at least part of that plan worked out!

My first job was working for Boeing on their F/A-18 fighter jet program. I spent my days programming fighter jet software in assembly language and I loved it. The U.S. government decided to save some money and went looking for other countries to sell this plane to. This put me into an unfamiliar role: I started to negotiate with foreign military officials and I ended up having to participate in the negotiations for large international deals.

Time moved on and so did I. I found myself working for Siemens, the big German telecommunications company. They were making phone switches and selling them to the seven U.S. phone companies. The problem was that the switches were too complicated. When it came time to negotiate a deal with the customer, the sales teams struggled to create an effective negotiating strategy. I was called in to bridge the world between the product functionality and the business impacts as they related to the negotiations.

I've spent over 25 years working as a negotiator for both big companies and startups. This has given me an opportunity to learn what it takes to both plan and execute negotiations of all sizes. When it comes to negotiations, I've pretty much been there, done that.

I now live in Tampa Florida where I spend my time managing my consulting business, Blue Elephant Consulting, teaching college courses at the University of South Florida, and traveling to work with companies like yours to share the knowledge that I have about how to prepare for and execute successful negotiations.

I'm always available to answer questions and I can be reached at:

Dr. Jim Anderson
Blue Elephant Consulting
Email: jim@BlueElephantConsulting.com
Facebook: http://goo.gl/1TVoK
Web: http://www.BlueElephantConsulting.com/

**"Unforgettable communication skills that will
set your ideas free..."**

Create An Effective Negotiating Team At Your Company!

Dr. Jim Anderson is available to provide training and coaching on the topics that are the most important to people who have to negotiate: how can my team effectively prepare for and execute a successful negotiation that will get us what we both want and need?

Dr. Anderson believes that in order to both learn and remember what he says, audiences need to laugh. Each one of his speeches is full of fun and humor so that what he says "sticks" with everyone.

Dr. Anderson's Negotiating Training Includes:

1. How to plan for a negotiation: what information do you need and where can you find it?

2. What's the best way to explore how a deal can be created during a negotiation?

3. How can you bring a negotiation to a close without giving in to the other side?

Dr. Jim Anderson works with over 100 customers per year. To invite Dr. Anderson to work with you, contact him at:

Phone: 813-418-6970 or
Email: jim@BlueElephantConsulting.com

Blue
Elephant
Consulting

Speaking. Negotiating. Managing. Marketing.

Chapter 1

Let's Get Physical

Let's Get Physical

This might fall into the "duh" category; however, you would not believe how many times even the most experienced CEOs forget that before you negotiate, you must be mentally and physically in the right place. This is just a fancy way of saying that you have to be very comfortable to negotiate. Physical and mental comfort as you negotiate is vastly underrated as a strategy.

Negotiating starts with being relatively comfortable. I shouldn't have to say it, but it's good to remember that you shouldn't negotiate the day after a loss in the family, you should wear comfortable clothes, whatever you do don't wear clothes that will make you feel inferior, (ladies especially) should not wear uncomfortable new shoes.

In his book Negotiate and Win, Dominick Misino tells the story about a negotiating team responded to a domestic-type dispute in a suburban neighborhood. A man had barricaded himself in a house for some trivial reason and was refusing to come out. No weapons had been seen and there was some question among the police officers as to whether the man was really barricading himself in the at all.

The negotiator said "I can deal with this easy." It was an early fall afternoon in the Northeast, one of those gorgeous 70 degree days just before the leaves start changing colors. The negotiator figured that he'd have the guy out in a few minutes and get back in time to know off early for dinner. Except that the person in the house turned out to be pretty serious about not coming out. And he turned out to have a weapon that no one had known about.

The afternoon turned into the evening and the evening into nighttime. The temperature dropped to 50 degrees and then dipped to 45. The negotiator, still in shirtsleeves, felt like he was freezing body parts off. By the time the man in the house finally agreed to come out, the negotiator was almost suffering from hypothermia.

He should have known better! Let all of us CEOs learn from this and make sure that we'll be comfortable no matter how long the negotiations go on.

Chapter 2

It's All About Power

It's All About Power

One of the big challenges to doing a good job of negotiating is that often you don't feel in control of the situation — you believe that the other side has all of the power. This of course is not true, because if it was then they would not be preparing to negotiate with you. They would just tell you what to do and you would do it. See? Now doesn't that make you feel better?

So here's a secret: power is not real. It only exists in your mind and so it is what you think it is. If you think that you are powerful, then you are. If you don't think that you are powerful, then you won't be. Sales people have known for a long time that negotiation is a process of information discovery. During this discovery process you learn what your sources of power for this particular negotiation are.

A long time ago, a negotiation researcher named Dr. Chester L. Karrass discovered that power is simply a state of mind. Those who think that they are powerless will negotiate weakly even if in reality they do have power. Those who think that they have power will negotiate from strength even if they really don't have any power.

The take away here is to get yourself in the right state of mind BEFORE you start to negotiate. Once you start the negotiations make sure that you keep your ears open so that you can discover your real sources of power. Then go out and make it happen!

Chapter 3

The Seven Deadly Sins Of Preparing To Negotiate

The Seven Deadly Sins Of Preparing To Negotiate

You wouldn't show up for a job interview naked (well, let's say that you wouldn't show up naked for MOST job interviews). You wouldn't sit down to gamble in Las Vegas unless you knew the rules of the game. You wouldn't start to run a marathon while wearing snow boots. So why would you ever even dream about starting a negotiation with a bunch of wrong assumptions?

You would be amazed at how many people actually do this. Somehow we have all talked ourselves into believing a lot of stuff about how negotiating is done and just who has the negotiating power that are flat out wrong. We seem to get ourselves off track even before we start to negotiate. How about if we spend some time now and identify these Seven Deadly Sins so that we can stop doing them!

1. **We assume that the other party is all-powerful and is holding all the cards**.

   Fact: In truth, the other side rarely, if ever, is all-powerful or has all of the cards. Instead at the start of a negotiation, power is shared by both sides. Perhaps not equally, but you always do have some power.

2. **The other side has a clear idea of exactly he wants.**

   Fact: Sometimes he does, sometimes he doesn't, no matter how detailed he may have been in describing what he is looking for before the negotiations begin. Often times, the other side has a lot of details about something that won't fix their problems. It's your job as a part of the negotiation process to listen and discover their true issues.

17

3. **The other side is only concerned about price.**

   Fact: price is the most overrated word in negotiation. It is an important part of the whole negotiation; however, it's not nearly as big of a deal as most people make it out to be. There are lots of other issues that need to be discussed and these issues will diminish the importance of price in the final agreement.

4. **There are other people / companies / products that have a better solution to offer the other side than you do.**

   Fact: This is almost always never the case. Of course there are other options for the other side no matter if you are talking about going on a date or buying an airplane. However, every single other option has an upside and a down side associated with it. What you bring the table has an upside and a down side also. Now the only thing to negotiate about is how valuable your upside it to the other side.

5. **You'd be in a better position to negotiate if only you had more authority.**

   Fact: In most negotiations, you'd be better off with less authority. Less authority means that you can build better relationships with the other side because you are NOT the decision maker, instead you are both in this together trying to come up with an agreement that "they" will accept.

6. **Your only real weapon is the ability to ask for less.**

   Fact: Asking for less is only one of the literally dozens of negotiation tools at your command, and, oh by the way, many are much more effective than asking for less.

7. **<u>You treat negotiating like just another meeting.</u>**

    <u>Fact</u>: failing to get enough sleep, do your homework, or wear comfortable clothing all provide the other side with power over you. Why would you ever put yourself at a disadvantage just because you didn't take the time to prepare?

There you go — now you know the 7 deadly sins that can diminish your negotiating power even before you start to negotiate. Overcoming these 7 can be challenging; however, learning to do so will start paying you back right off the bat.

Chapter 4

Don't Give
The Bad Guy A Gun

Don't Give The Bad Guy A Gun

Police hostage negotiatorss have a set of basic rules that they follow. One of the key ones is that no matter how strongly the bad guys might demand it, they NEVER give them a gun.

Seems like sorta a no-brainer, et? However, in the heat of negotiations nothing is ever that clear. The police know that if the bad guys threaten to harm hostages unless they get guns, there is always the possibility that someone might say "yes" and turn a bad situation into a worst situation. That's why they have all agreed on this rule long before they show up on site.

We can all learn from folks who negotiate every day. What they are telling us is that before starting any negotiation, you need to decide the specific goal that you want these negotiations to achieve and you need to decide what is negotiable and what is not.

This is called setting your negotiating parameters: know your "out" and your "push". The "out" is your best alternative – if the negotiations don't work out, then what are you going to do? The "push" is the approach that you are going to take: how hard and what buttons are you going to push?

Another key point that too many of us forget time after time is that we begin negotiating when we're still gathering information. Negotiations don't begin until you've gathered all of the information. Then it's time for you to sit back, evaluate the data that you've collected and work out what your "out" and "push" are.

The Boy Scouts got this right a long time ago: prepare, prepare, prepare.

Chapter 5

Deals That Make Money: How To Plan Your Concession

Deals That Make Money: How To Plan Your Concession

When negotiating deals with someone, you need to realize that they aren't just going to roll over and give you everything that you ask for. Instead, they are going to expect you to participate in a back-and-forth, give-and-take discussion in which both sides are expected to both concede as well as gain issues. This means that you need to have a strategy for each concession that you plan on offering to the other side. Looks like this calls for some serious planning!

First, let's make sure that we all understand why we are willing to make a concession. There are two reasons that you'd make a concession during a negotiation. First, to persuade the other side to move us close to a deal or to avoid a deadlock. Secondly, to increase the other side's satisfaction. Both of these reasons provide a powerful motivation to make concessions during the negotiation when it makes sense.

There are actually a great number of nuances to the best management of concessions; however, here are the four most important approaches that you should start to use immediately:

1. **Leave Yourself Lots Of Room (to Negotiate)**: Remember that a concession is a tool that is designed to help you move the negotiation along. If you leave yourself a great deal of "wiggle room" then you find that you'll have more room in which to use your concession tools.

2. **A Concession Should Be Given Slowly — Be Stingy!**: So much of the process of managing a concession has to do with managing the psychology of the other side. If you are too quick to offer a concession, then the other side will give it little value. If instead, they feel that they had

to work hard to get you to offer the concession, then they will highly value this hard won success.

3. **A.I.R.: Ask for something In Return.**: This is a subtle one, but you need to make sure that you clearly communicate that during the negotiation, nothing is for free. This means that every time you make a concession, you need to ask the other side for something in return. The challenge comes because you don't want to be seen as conducting a 1-for-1 negotiation. Instead, you'd like to be seen as more casual and carefree. However, deep down inside you need to be tracking all concessions and making sure that you've gotten something in return for everything that you've given up.

4. **Watch Your Rate Of Concessions**: Yes you will end up making several concessions during a normal negotiation. However, you need to make sure that you space these concessions out and don't bunch them together. Otherwise it will look like you are willing to give up more than you are. Especially be careful about what happens as you approach the end of the negotiation. Studies have shown that 80% of the concessions that are made are made in the last 20% of the negotiation time. Don't let deadlines cause you to make too many concessions!

There you have it. Using these four guidelines, you can turn a concession from an admission of negotiating weakness into a powerful tool for reaching the deal that you want.

Chapter 6

Make More Sales: Understanding Buyer Power & What To Do About It

Make More Sales: Understanding Buyer Power & What To Do About It

So you want to sell something (perhaps yourself for a new job?) and you feel that the other side (the buyer) has all the power. Ok, you're right – just give up and stop reading right now.

Hmm, you're still reading. Perhaps although it looks like the buyer has all the power, this really is not the case. Let's take a careful look at what is really going on here and perhaps we can boost your self-confidence just a bit.

First a quick review is probably called for. In negotiating, power is all in your head. We imagine that there are many sources of power and they can be based on resources, regulations, laws, or even psychological factors. In the end, we all have different views of just exactly what power means. Most of these views only exist in our heads and they form a critical part of what can be called our inner reality.

Given all that, what can we as a seller in a negotiation do to minimize the buyer's power while maximizing our own? Let's take a look at common sources of power and see how we can gain the upper hand:

- **Organizational Time**: the buyer may be under the gun because he/she needs what we have to sell in order to meet a demand that his organization is putting on him: "Fill that position NOW!"

- **Personal Time**: the buyer may have poor time management skills and has painted himself into a corner so that he needs to make a purchase NOW!

- **Specifications**: the product that you are offering (yes, even if it's just you) may be the only one that fits the requirements that he's trying to fill.

- **Location**: the closer your product is to where the customer needs it to be the better.

- **Re-Validation**: does the buyer have the time/energy/budget to re-validate another supplier if he doesn't select your product?

- **Warranty**: does your product come with a better warranty than any other offers that the buyer has?

In any negotiating situation not all of these sources of power are going to be valid. However, I'm willing to bet you that at least some of them will be. If you spend just a bit of time thinking about it before you enter into a situation where you are going to be selling something, I think that you'll find that you really have much more power than you thought that you did!

Chapter 7

NASA's Guide To Negotiation Goal Setting: Aim For The Moon!

NASA's Guide To Negotiation Goal Setting: Aim For The Moon!

What does it take to be successful in a negotiation? Long before you start doing any of the standard negotiation preparation tasks, you need to take just a moment and decide where you are aiming to get to. Although it sounds simple, all too often we enter into a negotiation with only a vague understanding of what it's going to take in order for us to be able to walk away with a feeling of success.

There is a danger to setting an overall goal for the negotiations – how will we feel if we don't achieve it? Really smart social scientists have been studying things like this for a long time and they've learned that setting such a goal will do two things for us: it will form an internal commitment to achieving the goal and it will set us up to feel a sense of ego loss if we end up not achieving it.

Sounds dangerous doesn't it?

A critical point that you need to realize is that everything that happens at the negotiating table is part of a feedback loop. The feedback that you receive while negotiating will either alter or reinforce your sense of being able to achieve your goal. Those smart scientists have discovered that we respond to the feedback that we're getting in the following ways:

- Our expectations of being able to achieve our goal go up after a negotiating success and, of course, they go down after a failure.

- If we think that we control our own success or failure, then our expectation are even more likely to go up and down.

- BIG successes lead to a sense of being able to accomplish our goal; BIG failures lead to a feeling of never being able to accomplish our goal.

- If your goal is either too easy to get to or too hard to achieve during the negotiations, then you won't feel much of anything – either success or failure.

If all it took to achieve your overall goal in negotiating was to have a highly placed goal, then we'd all be able to be successful each time we sat down to negotiate. However, life doesn't work out that way. The reason for this is because of the other side of the table – they are actively working against you!

The other side of the table has a specific set of tactics that they use to bring you down and lower your feeling of being able to accomplish your goal. Their tactics have names such as the Bogey, the Krunch, and the Nibble. If you had no defenses against these tactics, then the other side would win each time. That doesn't have to be the case and you always need to keep in mind that you have more power than you think that you do. Pick your negotiating goals carefully and make sure that they are going to motivate you and not hold you back.

Chapter 8

No Ha, Ha At Tata – Negotiation Over Land & A Car Plant

No Ha, Ha At Tata – Negotiation Over Land & A Car Plant

Negotiation is a skill that is used every day, all around the world. There's a great example of just how careful one must be when negotiating – remember, as Yogi Berra said "It's not over until it's over". Tata Motors thought that they had successfully negotiated a deal until it started to come undone. Let's take a look at what happened and see if there are any lessons to be learned here.

Tata Motors Ltd is part of the enormous Indian Tata Group company. Awhile back the eyes of the world were on Tata Motors because they had announced that they are going to be building a car called the Nano which was expected to be the world's most inexpensive car priced at $2,500. The car was scheduled to be launched in October of 2008.

Tata Motors had decided to build their car in India's state of West Bengal which is located in eastern India. West Bengal is an economically poor part of India and the arrival of a large car manufacturing operation was viewed by many as a very good thing. Tata Motors negotiated with the West Bengal government in order to obtain the 1,000 acres of land that was needed to build the plant and the shops for their suppliers. The local government obtained the land, signed a deal with Tata Motors and construction was started. End of story right? Nope, not by a long shot.

It turns out that the land for the auto plant used to be farmland. The West Bengal government says that they paid the affected farmers in most cases and legally seized the land in a few cases. The issue is that the farmers don't see it that way! In fact about 400 of the 1,000 acres are in dispute. So what did the farmers do? Simple, they demonstrated and got violent. Construction on the auto plant came to a halt. As though this wasn't bad enough, Tata Motors said that if the issue was not resolved, then they would move their auto plant to a different Indian state.

What's a local government to do? The West Bengal Governor sat down with the leader of the protests (who also happens to be the head of a local political rival to the current West Bengal government) and started to negotiate. After three days of negotiation, a compromise was reached. The exact deals of the compromise have not been released yet; however, the government has stated that they will try to return some of the land that had been forcibly taken from the farmers.

So what is to be learned from all of these international events? Ultimately, you need to do your homework and make sure that the parties that you are negotiation with have the power to deliver what they are promising. In this case Tata Motors relied on the West Bengal government to deliver land and it turns out that the land was not theirs to give. What could Tata Motors have done differently?

They could have split the negotiations into two parts: various permissions and incentives from the local government and buying the land directly from the farmers. This would have been more time consuming; however, it would have prevented the turmoil and the delays that resulted from assuming that the local government had the power to provide the land.

Chapter 9

The Power Of Planning Your Next Negotiation

The Power Of Planning Your Next Negotiation

Your parents, teachers, best friends, financial planners, parole officers, etc. were all right when they told you that in order to be successful in life you really need to plan, plan, plan. In the world of business, planning is a part of almost all activities; however, it's in the area of negotiations that business planning will provide you with the greatest return on your investment of time.

With all of this being said, you would think that planning would be second nature to anyone who is getting ready to enter into negotiations. You would be wrong.

It's not so much that folks forget to research the other side of the table (Google has made that easy to do almost instantaneously), but rather that we don't spend enough time understanding what WE are trying to get out of the negotiating.

The following steps will help you to put together a great plan for your next negotiating session:

Pick A Good Negotiator

Maybe the negotiator is you, but if it isn't, then make sure that you pick someone who know how to negotiate. Included in this person's set of skills should be a strong ability to work with teams and the ability to control their emotions.

Plug In To Your Power Sources

The key to having a successful negotiation is to make sure that you are negotiating from a source of power – hopefully a more powerful position than the other side of the table. This means that you need to take the time to identify your sources of power.

Remember that we always have MORE power than we initially think that we do. Additionally, study the other side's sources of power also. They almost always have LESS power than we initially think that they do.

One Night Stands vs. Long Term Relationships

Are you preparing to negotiate with someone that you will end up having a long-term relationship with? If so, then this means that you have not only short-term goals, but also long-term goals that need to be considered.

Why Are They Willing To Negotiate?

Making sure that you truly understand why the other side of the table is there in the first place can be the key to creating a solution that works for all. If you can uncover what their motivation is, then you have solved half of the problem of creating a solution that will work for both of you.

Goals Are Good

Knowing what motivates you is just as important as understanding the other side's motivation. You need to further understand what it's going to take in order for you to leave the negotiations feeling satisfied. This means that you need to have very clear goals so that you'll know when you have reached them.

Become A Time Lord

One hidden aspect of any negotiation is that everything changes. The things that we are negotiating for have had a value in the past, they have a different value today, and they'll have yet another value sometime off in the future. We need to be able to realize this and consider all three values when we are negotiating for something.

There you have it – the basic building blocks that need to go into the planning that you do for your next negotiating session. With these taken care of, you're almost guaranteed to be successful!

Chapter 10

How To Hire A Negotiator

NOW
HIRING

How To Hire A Negotiator

In life, there are some situations that you will be called on to negotiate in order to get what you want / need. However, there will also be situations in which you have the time (and the budget!) to reach out and get outside help.

Getting outside negotiating help can be especially critical if the type of negotiation that you are preparing to start is of a very technical or detailed nature. If you can find someone who has "been there, done that" you can significantly improve the odds of being successful in the negotiations. Now the big question is just how does one go about hiring a negotiator?

The challenge in interviewing someone to do negotiating on your behalf is that negotiation is a very difficult job to do. The reason that negotiating is such a challenge is because it doesn't just require one or two specific skills, but rather a whole collection of skills that we really don't find in business.

At a very high level, a good negotiator has the ability to show good business sense while at the same time displaying a deep understanding of how people think and act. It is a rare thing indeed to find both of these qualities in a single individual. Couple that with any special knowledge or experience that you are looking for and choosing the wrong CEO to represent you can appear to be all too easy.

The following 10 characteristics of a good negotiator are what you should be looking for when you are interviewing possible candidates. It's going to take some probing on your part to uncover these traits, but it will be worth the effort:

1. Must have the ability to negotiate well with members of YOUR team. If the candidate can't win the confidence of your team, how can you expect him to succeed in the

negotiation with the other side?

2. Must show that he/she has the ability to construct a plan and the commitment to follow it through. The ability to realize that not all information may be available before the negotiation starts and the willingness to check facts and alter plans as new details emerge are also critical.

3. Did I mention the need for sound business sense? The ability to see through the fog of negotiations and identify the issues that will have an impact on your bottom line is key.

4. The ability to deal with both ambiguity (both before and during the negotiations) as well as conflict during the actual negotiations.

5. The willingness to aim high when setting goals for the negotiations.

6. The ability to realize that a negotiation is a process and having the patience to wait for the other side to reveal more so that the process can move forward.

7. The ability to personally connect with both your team and the other side. Yes, negotiation is a business process, but the personal touch can make all the difference when it comes to closing the deal.

8. A realization that his / her personal integrity is what matters above all else.

9. The ability to, no matter how heated a discussion gets, listen with an open mind to what the other side is saying.

10. The self-confidence that is needed to see a negotiation through from start to finish.

Chapter 11

Single vs Team Negotiation: Which Is Better?

Single vs Team Negotiation: Which Is Better?

Sorry – that's a trick question. Most of the time when we talk about negotiating skills, we talk about how you can improve how YOU negotiate. However, in the real world, negotiations are often done by teams of senior executives.

The reasons for this are fairly simple: negotiations more often than not can take a long time and just the physical strain of active negotiating can wear a single person down quickly. Additionally, often special subject matter knowledge is required in order to hammer out specific issues and no one person possess all of that information. It takes a team to negotiate well.

There is, of course, one additional reason for preferring to negotiate using a team instead of a lone individual. During a negotiation so much is happening that a single individual is often hard pressed to stay on top of all of it.

Using a team for your negotiations allows you to use a group of people to capture all that is occurring. You can also use the team to jointly review what has transpired and make better decisions.

However, there are also several reasons for not wanting to use a team as a part of a negotiation process. Here are three of them:

- **Requires Coordination:** When you are the sole negotiator, once you know what you want to accomplish and how you are going to make it happen, then you are set. However, if you have a team of negotiators, then you need to make sure that everyone on your team REALLY understands what the goals are. This can be a challenge to do, especially if your goals change during the negotiation.

- **Sharing Information:** In order for a team of CEOs to work together successfully, they need to all be aware of the same information. This will require that all information about the negotiation be collected, shared, and reviewed prior to the start of the negotiations. This can be a challenge under the best of circumstances and if the team is geographically distributed then it becomes even more difficult.

- **Showing Disunity:** In the end, negotiating is all about power. Having team members become confused or showing disunity will reduce your power and increase the other side's power.

With all that being said, you would think that nobody would ever use a team to perform a negotiation. However, you would be wrong. There are a number of compelling reasons why teams should be used more often for negotiations than they currently are:

- **Better Coordination:** Using a team allows you to distribute the tasks of negotiating among team members. This means that documents that need to be produced or facts that need to be checked can be done in parallel to the negotiations and this will speed the process up and reduce confusion.

- **More Experts:** A single CEO can only provide his / her expertise to the negotiations. A team can provide a much broader collection of experts and this should help the discussions move much faster.

- **Moral Support:** Since a negotiation can continue for a long time, it's easy to become disheartened if it appears as though an agreement will never be reached. If you are working with a team, it will be must easier to "keep a stiff upper lip" and not give up.

- **Listen Better:** One set of ears can only hear so much. In fact, not only can multiple ears simply hear better, but they can also hear things differently which might help the negotiation move along faster.

- **Plan Better:** A plan that is created by a single CEO is as good as that CEO. A plan that is created by multiple negotiators is often much better because it reflects the different inputs of multiple people.

Chapter 12

Should CEOs Be In Long Term Relationships?

Should CEOs Be In Long Term Relationships?

Who wouldn't want to be in a **long term relationship**? I mean we wanted our parents to be in one, we want to be in one, movies always end by having the hero walk off into the sunset and into a long term relationship, right?

It turns out (as with so many things in life), when it comes to sales negotiations it depends on what side of the table that you're sitting on as to if you should want to be in a long term relationship...

Let's be straight here, getting ourselves into a long term relationship makes life sooo much easier. There are all sorts of **benefits** like reliability, friendship, and even peace of mind. However, it has been shown that over time these types of relationships start to favor one party over the other. Here's what can happen:

- You can lose your objectivity
- You can become compliant
- You can lose your company's secrecy
- You can become too dependent on the other side

If you are a seller, then getting into a long term relationship can be a very good thing. Generally speaking, **long term relationships favor the seller over the buyer**. Here's why:

- More often than not, product specifications change over time.

- Changes in product specifications tend to increase the seller's margin.

- The seller can tailor standard offerings into special products and charge more for them.

The seller has fuller access to the buyer's organization – the reverse is not true.

Sure seems like the seller has an unfair advantage doesn't it? Buyers should take heart, there are actually a **number of things that a buyer can do** to even the score:

- Change buyers every few years just to shake things up.

- Expand the number of competitors vying to be your supplier.

- Have another group evaluate each long term relationship every so often.

Long term relationships do have their advantages; however, just as with your love life, you need to step back every so often and make sure that this relationship is **the right for you right now**.

Hard work does not
guarantee success;
However, success does
not happen
without hard work.

- Dr. Jim Anderson

Create An Effective Negotiating Team At Your Company!

Dr. Jim Anderson is available to provide training and coaching on the topics that are the most important to people who have to negotiate: how can my team effectively prepare for and execute a successful negotiation that will get us what we both want and need?

Dr. Anderson believes that in order to both learn and remember what he says, audiences need to laugh. Each one of his speeches is full of fun and humor so that what he says "sticks" with everyone.

Dr. Anderson's Negotiating Training Includes:

1. How to plan for a negotiation: what information do you need and where can you find it?

2. What's the best way to explore how a deal can be created during a negotiation?

3. How can you bring a negotiation to a close without giving in to the other side?

Dr. Jim Anderson works with over 100 customers per year. To invite Dr. Anderson to work with you, contact him at:

Phone: 813-418-6970 or
Email: jim@BlueElephantConsulting.com

Blue
Elephant
Consulting

Speaking.   Negotiating.   Managing.   Marketing.

Photo Credits:

Cover - By: kris krüg
https://www.flickr.com/photos/kk/

Chapter 1 - By: Official U.S. Navy Imagery
http://www.flickr.com/photos/usnavy/

Chapter 2 - By: JAS_photo
http://www.flickr.com/photos/jas_fauxtoes/

Chapter 3 - By: Ken Yu
http://www.flickr.com/photos/kenudigit/

Chapter 4 - By: DieselDemon
http://www.flickr.com/photos/28096801@N05/

Chapter 5 - By: Frits Ahlefeldt-Laurvig
http://www.flickr.com/photos/hikingartist/

Chapter 6 - By: International Institute of Tropical Agriculture
http://www.flickr.com/photos/iita-media-library/

Chapter 7 - By: NASA's Marshall Space Flight Center
http://www.flickr.com/photos/nasamarshall/

Chapter 8 - By: Porschista
http://www.flickr.com/photos/porschista/

Chapter 9 - By: Community Eye Health
http://www.flickr.com/photos/communityeyehealth/

Chapter 10 - By: Nathan Stephens
http://www.flickr.com/photos/groundswellzoo/

Chapter 11 - By: Marc
http://www.flickr.com/photos/sumofmarc/

Chapter 12 - By: Seranya Photography
http://www.flickr.com/photos/seranyaphotography/

What You Need To Do BEFORE A Negotiation Starts In Order To Get The Best Possible Outcome

This book has been written with one goal in mind – to show you how to prepare to be successful during your next negotiation. It's not easy being a negotiator and so we're going to show you what you need to be doing before the negotiation starts in order to get the deal that you want!

Let's Make Your Negotiation A Success!

What You'll Find Inside:

- **THE 7 DEADLY SINS OF PREPARING TO NEGOTIATE**

- **DEALS THAT MAKE MONEY: HOW TO PLAN YOUR CONCESSIONS**

- **MAKE MORE SALES: UNDERSTANDING BUYER POWER & WHAT TO DO ABOUT IT**

- **SINGLE VS TEAM NEGOTIATION: WHICH IS BETTER?**

Dr. Jim Anderson brings his 25 years of real-world experience to this book. He's been a negotiator at some of the world's largest firms. He's going to show you what you need to do (and not do!) in order to get the best deal out of your next negotiation!